The Race Toward Collaboration:
10 Rules For Parents to Engage With Schools

Timothy King Sr.: Crowning Moments
2016

Dedication

I would like to dedicate this manual to my mom, Vernetta J. King. You instilled in me a love of learning that will never fade. Thank you for dreaming for me before I had dreams of my own.

The Race Toward Collaboration:
10 Rules For Parents to Engage With Schools

© 2016 by Timothy King. All rights reserved.
No part of this publication may be reproduced, stored in or introduced into a retrieval system, or transmitted, in any form or by any means (electronic, mechanical, photocopying, recording or otherwise), without the prior written permission of the copyright owner, except by a reviewer who may quote brief passages in a review.

First Printing: 2016

Crowning Moments
PO Box 352504
Palm Coast, FL 32135

www.crowningmomentsconsultants.com

Table of Contents

Introduction..1

The Start..2

Rule 1: Be Visible 4

Rule 2: Be Available..6

Rule 3: Be Present 8

The Distance 10

Rule 4: Know The Rules 13

Rule 5: Talk 15

Rule 6: Listen with a Purpose 17

Rule 7: Ask Questions 19

The Finish 21

Rule 8: Share The Goal 25

Rule 9: Seek Help 27

Rule 10: Don't Give Up 29

Parental Supports 31

Parental Resources 32

References 36

Introduction

Every parent wants to see his or her child achieve academic success. The problem is, often as parents, it's difficult to know where to look for help. This manual will walk you through parental involvement from an administrator's point of view with the goal of building knowledge with 10 working rules for every parent to effectively participate in the educational decisions for their child.

Current research reveals to us the importance of parental involvement. A 2002 study, by the Southwest Development Laboratory on parent involvement over the past 10 years, revealed that regardless of family income or background, students with involved parents are more likely to:

◦ Earn higher grades and test scores and enroll in higher-level programs
◦ Be promoted, pass their classes, and earn credits
◦ Attend school regularly
◦ Have better social skills, show improved behavior, and adapt well to school
◦ Graduate and go on to postsecondary education

(Henderson & Mapp, 2002)

This manual was written for parents who have students in K-12 Public Education systems. This manual will walk you through parental involvement using the elements of a race: The Start, The Distance, and The Finish. Each leg of the race should provide quality insight that will help you lead your child toward the finish line.

The Start

I had as many doubts as anyone else. Standing on the starting line, we're all cowards.
Alberto Salazar

Jade

Jade Smith is a 4th grade student at Brooks Elementary School. Jade has not struggled with academics or behavior. Her mother has never received a call from the school with a bad report. Recently, Jade was recognized for a Citizenship Award at school. The award was presented during the school assembly. Jade watched eagerly and waited with anticipation for her mother to show up. To her disappointment, her mother never showed up to see her receive the award. Her teacher, Mrs. Jenkins, saw the disappointment on her face as other children's guardians snapped pictures and made memories.

Near the end of the day, a woman enters the building and asks to speak with Mrs. Jenkins. When the receptionist asked for her ID, the lady replied, "I left it in the car, but I'm Jade's mom. I didn't know that I needed to bring it in with me." The receptionist asked, "Have you been here before?" Her mom replied, "No!" The receptionist patiently waited for mom to go and get her ID. With her ID in hand, Jade's mom returned to the desk and was given a pass to the classroom. She stood at the desk unsure of which way to go. With a map in hand, she walked the halls looking for her daughter's classroom. She stopped a few times with looks of confusion. Teachers in the halls helped and pointed her to the room. She peered into the room. To her surprise, Jade wasn't her usual self and had tears in her eyes. She quickly entered and introduced herself. As soon as Jade saw her mom, a smile sprung to her face! "You missed it, but you came," she yelled with excitement. "It's a pleasure to meet you Mrs. Smith," said Mrs. Jenkins. "Jade talks about you every day."

Rule # 1
Be Visible

If you showed up at your child's school today would they know you? Parents need to be visible in their child's school and educational decisions. Being visible on campus is a great start toward collaboration. Collaboration is when two or more people work together to achieve a goal. Teachers and school administrators rely on parental support, and seeing you will help them to put a face with a name that they'll call on later. Sometimes parental visibility can be difficult, but it can be accomplished with some work.

Our children see us invest in the things that are important to us. An easy way to show your child that you are fully invested in them and their school is to show up! Be the parent in the front row of the assembly. Be the parent who takes his or her lunch break to swing by school to check-in to see how things are going. Let your child see you on campus. Build face and name recognition on campus. Being visible is taking the extra 10 minutes to walk your child to class instead of dropping them off in the car rider line. Being visible is attending the awards ceremony. Being visible is meeting them at the bus stop. I'll tell you a secret; visible parents get special privileges. I'll explain. When your child is scheduled to attend a field trip and the chaperone list is full, who do you think gets to go? The parents who have been visible are more likely to be chosen than the parents that the teacher has not met or are never visible. Faceless parents have become too common. It's the voice on the other end of the phone, but the person you never get to meet. Remove excuses, and find a way to be visible.

Ways to be visible:

Meet the Teacher Day

Scheduled Parent Conference

Lunch Dates With Your Child In the School Cafeteria

Assist With and/or Attend School Assemblies

Join Parent Teacher Association/Parent Teacher Organization

Join School Advisory Committee

Join Watch DOGS (Dads of Great Students) or similar programs

Walk Your Child to Class

Pick-up and Drop-off at the bus stop or at school

Chaperone Field Trips

Rule # 2
Be Available

When was the last time you were available to help at school?

Being visible at school is a big first step. Now that we are out of the starting block, let's move to our next step. Be available. It's easy to confuse being visible with being available, but those words aren't used interchangeably. To be visible is to be seen and recognized, and to be available is to be willing to give time. Our lives move at 100 mph, and our schedules are constantly full. We often feel crunched for time, and usually there is none left to give. That is the reality of current society, but let me offer a counter view. A full calendar always has openings. Sometimes those openings aren't in the calendar's view of today, this week, or this month, but if you look, you will find an opening. This is a critical point. At the beginning of the year, every teacher or school releases a calendar of events. It's the perfect time to mark your calendar as available to help your child's teacher or school with a function.

Sometimes being available will mean sacrificing. Your child and your child's school will appreciate you sacrificing your time to be there! Let your child's teacher know you're availability. Move and rearrange your schedule when you can to make yourself available. Because you're visible, they (teachers and school staff) recognize you, and they will ask you for help. When they ask you for help, do your best to offer them a yes, or counter offer with a different date of availability? Find out the requirements for volunteering in your child's school district and get cleared. You are in control of your calendar and your time. Please make yourself available.

Ways to be available:

Schedule Time On Campus Early and Often
Use Technology To Help Organize Your Schedule/Time
Set Reminders
Communicate Your Availability
Make Helping a Priority
Organize
Be Flexible
Get a School Calendar
Get Cleared to Volunteer
Schedule/Lead an Event

Rule # 3
Be Present

Can you distinguish between being there and being present?

The first 10 meters out of the block are very important for runners. We are closing our first 10 meters with rule 3. Be present. It's vital that parents are present. Being present is the ability to be active in the moment. The classroom teacher and school would love for you to be an active participant in your child's learning. This will look different as your child changes grades and schools. The general expectation is that you as the parent be active in helping with homework and participating in school functions and events. To be present is to bypass the attitude of "I am here to be seen" and transitioning into the attitude of "I am here to be a part of what's happening." The attitude of a parent towards school and school involvement is a good measuring stick for being present.

Let's be honest. School may not always be the place that makes you smile, but knowing that you are working to help your child through their educational journey should put a smile on your face. As a parent who is present, you wield the power to advocate for your child and bring solutions to the table for improving the learning environment. Your role as a support system and helper for your child is intensified when you are present. The National Parent Teacher Association released a guide in 2002, suggesting that the most accurate predictor for student achievement was parental involvement. Parental involvement is easily defined as active engagement, which is further clarified as being present. Be visible. Be available. Be present.

Ways to Be Present:

Participate with a Good Attitude

Know the School Layout

Access the School's Website

Be a Reading Partner

Get Involved with School Policy Decision

Attend School Board Meetings

Participate in Career Day

Prepare Something for the Bake Sale

Help with After-school/Extra-curricular Activities

Contribute to the School's Parent Group

The Distance

The importance of parental involvement in children's education cannot be overstated.
Lisa Blair

Bill

Bill Johnson is a 10th grade student at Central High School. Bill has been a pretty good student that has some average grades and a few problems here and there with behavior. He likes school, and he is a sports star. Recently, Bill and his girlfriend broke up. Bill has struggled with this breakup, and he has had a couple of emotional meltdowns. Most occur during class change when he sees his ex-girlfriend talking to other guys. On Tuesday morning, Bill was at his locker when he saw his ex-girlfriend hugging his best friend. In a rage, Bill ran over to them. He shoved his ex-girlfriend to the floor and punched his best friend in the face. He then proceeded to yell obscenities towards the both of them. Mr. Wilson, a dean at Central, was in the hall and quickly responded to the incident. With Mr. Wilson present, Bill continued to yell and make threats to harm them when he sees them away from school. Mr. Wilson escorted Bill to the office.

Once Bill calmed down, Mr. Wilson asked him to recount the events that had taken place in the hallway. After hearing Bill's account of the events, Mr. Wilson told Bill that he was going to issue an out of school suspension. Mr. Wilson called Bill's Dad, Mr. Johnson, to make him aware of the incident, the consequences, and the supports available to him from the school. Mr. Johnson erupted on the phone and promised to be there in 10 minutes. As promised, Mr. Johnson arrived within 10 minutes and demanded to see Mr. Wilson immediately. Mr. Wilson invited Mr. Johnson into his office and began trying to finish the conversation that started on the phone. Mr. Johnson was enraged! He demanded that Mr. Wilson be considerate of his son's emotional state and that he not remove him from school. He further argued to Mr. Wilson that the school was simply picking on his son since football season was over. Mr. Wilson tried to explain that he was following the district's discipline procedures and that he was willing to offer in lieu of suspension options for Bill. Mr. Johnson continued to argue that he didn't want any suspension options. Mr. Johnson became verbally abusive toward Mr. Wilson and threatened to sue him if Bill was suspended. Mr. Wilson, again, tried to explain that he had to follow district policy, but that included reviewing in lieu of suspension options and building supports for Bill. Mr. Johnson stormed out of the office and barked at Bill to follow him.

Mr. Wilson drafted a letter to Mr. Johnson. The letter gave a summary of the incident that caused discipline action for Bill. It gave the suggested consequence as well as in lieu of suspension options. The letter also included supports for Bill, a referral to the district's mental health counselor to address peer conflict and anger management, and a change of schedule so that he wouldn't see his ex-girlfriend in the hallway.

The school social worker delivered the letter to Mr. Johnson that afternoon. He was still upset when she arrived, but he read the letter and immediately began to apologize to her. He wished that he had known, prior to this incident, the district's policy for discipline. He told her that when he became upset, he never stopped to listen. He asked her to let Mr. Wilson know that he wanted to use the in lieu of suspension option of community service to reduce the out of school suspension. He also signed the counseling referral for Bill. Mr. Johnson was surprised and excited that the school was willing to help and support Bill through this difficult time in his life.

Rule # 4
Know the Rules

Do you know school rules and policy is developed?

School systems across the United States all have to follow the same process for development of rules and policy. It all begins with federal laws. Federal laws give a wide range of do's and don'ts that each state has to follow. Sometimes there are slight differences in interpretations of those federal laws, but everyone follows the general principles of those laws. Next, each state develops their set of state laws. These state laws must be in compliance with federal laws. Once state laws are established, they are sent down to school districts. School districts must review these laws and develop school board policy based on the state laws. Once school board policy has been written, the district must produce a Student Code of Conduct that gives an outline of district policy and expectations for students' conduct. Schools develop school wide rules and expectations from the Student Code of Conduct. Classroom teachers develop their classroom rules and management system from the school wide rules and expectations.

When parents struggle with a discipline related rule at a school, it's important to know the source of that rule. Schools won't ever be able to change something that's in place because of federal law, but they can change a policy that was developed at the school level. As a parent, you have a powerful voice to advocate for change. Make sure you know your local board members and state representatives. They can impact policy and will impact policy if enough voters express their wishes and desires.

Ways to Know the Rules:

Be Active at Your Child's School

Contact Your Local Congressman

Contact Your State Senator

Contact Your Local School Board Representatives

Visit Your District's Website (School Board Policies are there)

Ask to be a Member of District Review teams

Attend School Board Meetings

Participate in Developing the Student Code of Conduct

Be on Alert for Updates from your District

Attend District Town Hall Meetings

Rule # 5
Talk

Is talking a part of your communication skill set?

Communication is an important part of any relationship. The relationship between home and school is no different than other relationships; without communication, it will die. Communication can be simply defined as an exchange of information between two parties. The United States is a diverse nation, composed of many cultural and ethnic identities. We are born with some communication skills, and some communication skills we have to learn. As simply as talking sounds, it's sometimes very difficult. In the heat of moment, when we have an opposing view, our adrenaline kicks in, and our voice starts to rise. Some times the rate of our speech increases. Without even knowing or trying, we have moved beyond talking and begin to yell.

Yelling isn't an effective form of communication, even though it's the most common way we communicate when we're upset. You can be passionate, and you should be passionate about your child. Nevertheless, it's very important to communicate those feelings and emotions through meaningful conversation. Through conversation, parents have the ability to advocate (speak on behalf on your child) and to negotiate (find a compromise). A parent's ability to talk to teachers and administrators helps to quickly find resolutions to difficult problems on campus. When preparing to address an issue or speak with someone, it's ok to review what you want to say and write it down. You can use it as a guide as you're talking. At the end of the day, your child should have you as their primary advocate.

Ways to Talk:

Ask for a Face-to-Face Meeting
Ask for a Phone Conference
Brainstorm Questions before the Meeting
Compose Emails (Read twice before sending)
Write a Note to the Teacher (Read twice before sending)
Be Prepared to Offer Solutions
Be Prepared to Accept Varied Responses
Respond to Opportunities for Parent Input (Surveys and etc.)
If Needed, Ask for an Interpreter to be Present
Use Technology as a Bridge Between Home and School

Rule # 6
Listen

When others are talking, are you listening?

To effectively communicate, one must not only be willing to talk, but you must also be willing to listen. Listening should not be confused with hearing. Hearing is the ability to recognize sounds. We all hate it when people hear us but do not listen to us. Listening is the ability to process and categorize sounds in preparation to respond. Listening is an active process even though it seems passive. When dealing with schools, listening is just as important as talking. Communication should be shared and meaningful. It should be a combination of talking and listening. The exchange between you and school staff will be a give and take. If you aren't listening, then you could miss a school's genuine attempt to help support your child or reach an agreeable resolution with you.

Hostile situations lead to heated discussions. In those heated instants, we must do our very best to listen to what's being said to us. Without listening, we aren't communicating; we're simply giving information with no way to know if it's being received. If our talking isn't being received, then it's ineffective. Ineffective communication leads to frustration as well as unresolved issues and complaints. When listening to others, it becomes clear on which pieces of information needs further clarification and which pieces of information are common points of agreement. With effective listening skills, you'll be able to navigate through conversations with school staff and reach the best possible outcomes for your child.

Ways to Listen:

Be Attentive

Have an Open Mind

Listen to Phone Messages from School

Read All Communications from School

Express When You Aren't Being Heard

Be Clear With Your Information

Attend Parent Nights

Establish an Effective Communication Vehicle

Give Positive Feedback

End Negative Communication With School Staff

Rule # 7
Ask Questions

How often do you ask questions when you don't understand?

Currently there are 1.17 Billion Google users, and Google users enter 40,000 search queries a second. Those numbers are mind blowing! With numbers that high, it would seem that our society is always asking questions, but that's not the case with parents and schools. Asking a question is the last part of effective communication, but parents skip it frequently. There is great value in asking for information to be clarified. When you're meeting with school staff, be sure to ask questions so that you are clear on what's being communicated. You can save yourself a headache and an argument by knowing exactly what's being proposed and having a plan to address it.

Miscommunication between home and school is an avoidable issue that can be solved when the parties involved start to ask questions. Asking questions to clarify information is not the beginning to initiating an argument as some people believe, but it's the final piece to effective communication. It lets the sender of a message know that you received their message, and you're processing it to give a response. Your questions should not be asked as a "Gotcha moment", but they should have the genuine intent to further the conversation and reach a resolution. Sometimes questions will arise after a conversation has ended. That's ok. You can contact the school staff member you were speaking with and tell them you need to ask a question. Schools want parents to be involved. Asking questions helps to further your involvement and clears up miscommunication.

Ways and When to Ask Questions:

School Advisory Meeting

Open House

Parent/Teacher Conference

Parent Teacher Association/Organization Meeting

Town Hall Meetings

Curriculum Nights

School Webmail

Open Response Surveys

District Parent Committees

Initial Registration Time or Transfer/Change of Schools

The Finish

"Education is the great engine of personal development. It is through education that the daughter of a peasant can become a doctor, that a son of a mineworker can become the head of the mine, that a child of farm workers can become the president of a nation."

Nelson Mandela

The Doan Family

Mr. and Mrs. Doan are the proud parents of four beautiful children: Jasmine a 1st grader, Jeffrey a 3rd grader, Ashley an 8th grader, and Douglas an 11th grader. Both Mr. and Mrs. Doan work full-time jobs and do their best to be active parents. Life is busy in the Doan home with the kids being active in sports and community events, but things have slowed down since they relocated to a smaller town. The hustle and bustle of each day isn't what it used to be.

Recently, the Doan had dealt with some bad news. The family suffered a great lost with the passing of Mr. Doan's father, and the factory where Mrs. Doan works is being shut down. The grief of losing a loved one, coupled with the pending loss of Mrs. Doan's job, has weighed heavily on the kids. Teachers still learning the Doan's kids haven't had enough time to notice anything was wrong. Mr. and Mrs. Doan have seen a change in the kids' attitude and demeanor. Despite their best efforts to shoulder the burden of grief and the stress of finances, the kids have taken them on as their own. Jeffrey's teacher, Mr. Cruz was heart-broken when he read Jeffrey's journal:

December 10, 2013

My Christmas wish is that my grandpa would be alive. I loved spending time with grandpa. We would go fishing! Sometimes he would fall asleep in the chair while we were fishing, and I would hear him snore. But he would wake up and catch the fish. My second Christmas wish is that my mom gets a job. She is a good worker, and dad can't pay the bills by himself. If she doesn't have a job, then I don't think we will have a house. My last Christmas wish is that I don't repeat 3rd grade again. I really hope this wish comes true. I asked last year, but I wasn't smart enough to past the test. So I have to do it again this year.

Mr. Cruz wiped tears from his eyes. Jeffrey was new to their school this year, and the school had been unsuccessful in obtaining prior records. He reached out to the teachers of Jasmine, Ashley, and Douglas. He asked how the students were performing in class and shared Jeffrey's letter. Each teacher expressed that the students were struggling academically and none of them were aware of their grandfather's passing. Mr. Cruz thanked the teachers for speaking with him and set out to help.

    He called Mr. Doan and asked if he could schedule a parent conference. Mr. Doan told him he'd love to attend, but he's working as much overtime as he can right now. So he wouldn't be able to make a meeting. Mr. Cruz asked if Mrs. Doan could attend, and Mr. Doan told him that he would speak with her and see if she was available. The next day, Jeffrey brought a note from Ms. Doan stating that she could meet today at 5:00pm. Mr. Cruz called the other teachers and told him that mom was coming in for a conference. When 5:00 rolled around, Mrs. Doan was standing at the front office doors. She was tired and worn from a long day of working in the factory. Mr. Cruz greeted her, and they walked toward his room. As they were walking, she asked nervously if the kids had done something wrong. Mr. Cruz told her that Jeffrey had written a response in his journal that caught him off guard, and he wanted to be sure that the school was doing everything they could to help. He told her that he had spoken to the other children's teachers, and they had come to his class to meet together. She stopped in her tracks and told him that despite what he had read, they were a good family, and they had always found a way to help themselves. She didn't want any "handouts" or "people in their business". Mr. Cruz assured her that he didn't have any "hand-outs" for her and that he wasn't attempting to be "in her business". He simply wanted to help educate her children, which is his business.

When they entered the room, the other teachers introduced themselves. Mr. Cruz shared Jeffrey's journal. Immediately, tears began to run down her cheeks, and she could barely speak. She said grandpa had died nearly a year ago. They were offered grief counseling but never went. She said that Jeffrey had been retained in 3rd grade the year before. He had been a good, but, struggling student. When grandpa died, he didn't complete any work, and his grades started to fall. He then failed his state assessment. She wept loudly and said, "Jeffrey loved fishing, but he won't fish anymore." "It's too hard!"
The family moved to this area because jobs were scarce back home, and they wanted to see new scenery for the kids. They had hoped a new area would give better jobs and a chance to move on. Mr. Cruz outlined the district's tutoring support. The others teacher added additional ways to help and things to do that could help improve their academics. Lastly, she was given a grief support group's brochure. It was clear to Mrs. Doan that her and Mr. Doan's struggles were not her own. She made a choice that day to get the family the support and help they needed to move on.

Rule # 8
Share The Goal

Does your child's teacher know your expectations for learning?

Every parent has high expectations for their children. In some cases those expectations are expressed to teachers from parents, but more often than not, parents don't fully express their expectations and goals for their children. Having a shared goal puts everyone on the same page in working towards fulfilling the goal. To best serve your child, it's important that teachers know what you expect. One of the most frustrating experiences a teacher can have is to think that they are on the same page with a parent—only to find out that parent has not fully disclosed their expectations or goals for their child. The desire to have a shared goal works for the student's benefit and confirms the bond between home and school.

The disappointment of not having a clear goal can be found at every grade level but becomes much more noticeable at the secondary level. At the secondary level, students really start to make choices that lead to college and careers. The selection of courses and participation in extra-curricular activities becomes critical. When parents aren't working hand in hand with teachers and school staff, it's easy for students to be lost in transition. Students who are looking to immediately enter the workforce won't have the same approach as students who are looking to immediately attend college. Parents who are connected to the school and sharing their goal for their child have a greater chance to influence those decisions and be at the table as decisions are being made.

Ways to Share Your Goal:

Parent Conference

School Committees

Share Career Options You've Discussed

Participate in Career Day

Advocate for Specific Courses

Advocate for Extra-Curricular Choices and Activities

Promote College Tours/programs

Promote Vocational Options

Negotiate with Community Leaders for Programs in Schools

Provide Feedback to the District on Programs

Rule # 9
Solicit Help

Are you comfortable asking for help?

The relationship between home and school is only as good and as strong as communication is between you and the school. Schools are in the business of educating students, but they also understand that students won't achieve without some basic needs being met. When schools are unsure of those needs, it's hard to put students in the best position to learn. Home life factors weigh heavily in students learning. When parents take on stress, it inadvertently trickles down to their children. Learning becomes more difficult when stress is present. In the relationship with your child's school, it's important to know that you are on the same page with a common goal for your child. If you feel that your child needs additional support in reading, tell the teachers. If you feel that your child needs additional support in Science, tell the teachers. Whatever your goal is for your child, it has to be shared with school staff.

Don't withhold information from teachers that could help them develop supports that would put your child into a better position to learn. There has to be an initial level of trust in school staff to adequately meet the needs of your child. Schools can't meet those needs without knowing them. Ask for the help your child needs! Don't think the needs of your child are too small or too large for the school. Schools don't have all of the answers, but they are able to provide great supports to students on campus and in many cases can connect students and families to outside agencies for help. The last thing schools want to do is be in your business, but they want to educate your child, which is their business.

Ways to Solicit Help:

Ask About Support Programs

Complete Mutual Consent Forms

Sign Request for Evaluations For School

Request Counseling Support From School

Ask for Additional Materials To help With Academics And/Or Behavior

Connect With Parents Who Have Similar Concerns

Attend Meetings

Seek Help at District Level

Partner With Community Agencies

Ask About Academic and Behavior Interventions At School

Rule # 10
Don't Give Up

What do you do when you're too tired to keep going?

Don't give up! While advocating for your child can be tiresome, and navigating the various rules and policies can be difficult, you can't give up! The success of your child falls squarely on your shoulders. If you give up, who's going to be their advocate? Who's going to ask the tough questions and hold everyone accountable? The partnership between home and school can't exist if you walk away. There will be days of high frustration. There will be moments of complete and utter disappointment. Days like that are to be expected, but they can't stop you from being an active parent.

Research on student achievement indicates through numerous studies that the key ingredient for students to succeed is parental involvement. Your involvement in your child's education makes all the difference in the world. Your involvement supersedes your race, your ethnicity, your annual income, your marital status, your living conditions, and any potential barriers. It levels the playing field, and in many cases it will put your child ahead. You can't give up because your child needs you. Your child needs to know that you have their back. The school needs you. They need to know that you have their back. You are the irreplaceable and constant piece in the partnership between home and school. Your child will move through grades and schools, but you will always be their constant. Don't let the school down. Don't let your child down. Don't give up!

"Nothing you do for your children is ever wasted. They seem not to notice us, hovering, averting our eyes, and they seldom offer thanks, but what we do for them is never wasted" - Garrison Keillor

Ways to Not Give Up:

Participate in School Activities

Participate in District Activities

Join School Based Organizations

Advocate on Local and State Levels

Be Informed

Set Goals for Your Child and Track Them

Develop Community Partnerships

Explore New Educational Options

Provide Input to School and District on Topics of Interest

Host School Based Events

Parental Supports

NEA/PTA Parent Guides. *A series of 10 parent guides. Available at* www.nea.org/parents/parent-guides.html
Project Appleseed. Project Appleseed is a massive family and parental involvement campaign. Information is available at www.projectappleseed.org.
Parental Involvement. Below is a list of web-based references with information:
www.centerforpubliceducation.org/Main-Menu/Public-education/Parent-Involvement
www.studentprivacysymposium.org/assets/Beyond-the-Fear-Factor_Sep-2015.pdf
www.ldaamerica.org/parents/
www.education.nh.gov/instruction/school_health/health_coord_family.htm
www.scholastic.com/parents/

Additional Parental Involvement Opportunities

Let The Principal Know You Are Available To Help

Volunteer For School Committees

Organize and Volunteer for Food and Clothing Drives

Assist With Class and School Parties

Go and Volunteer For School Activities, Sports, and/or Clubs

Participate in Bake Sales

Attend Parent Nights

Meet the Principal, Counselors, and Teacher

Ask For A Copy of The Student Code of Conduct From your Child's Teacher, School, and/or District

Parental Resources

Mutual Consent Form
The following form is available for download at
www.crowningmomentsconsultants.com

MUTUAL EXCHANGE OF INFORMATION

Date: _____
Concerning:
Student: _____
DOB: ___/___/____
Last First Middle
School attending: _____

I, parent or guardian, do hereby authorize the mutual exchange of medical, psychiatric, social work, psychological, educational records, and developmental history information regarding the above named student between:

Name:
Address:
Contact
And

_____County Schools

SCHOOL: _____
ADDRESS: _____

The purpose of this information is to ensure that the educational program offered to your child is of the best possible quality. It may be used in making recommendations regarding educational placement, but no decisions will be final without separate consent. I understand that I may revoke this consent at any time except to the extent that action based on this consent has been taken.

This authorization is fully understood and is made voluntarily on my part.

PARENT OR LEGAL GUARDIAN:
Signature: _____
Address: _____
Telephone: _____

Parent Conference Request
The following form is available for download at
www.crowningmomentsconsultants.com

Dear _____

I am requesting a parent conference to address my concerns. I have

concerns in the areas of _____.

I'm available to conference on _____. If that date and time

is not available, please call me at _____ so that we can discuss

the earliest date available.

Sincerely,

Records Request
The following form is available for download at
www.crowningmomentsconsultants.com

Dear _____,
I am requesting that a copy of the items listed below be made available for pickup within 72 hours.
School:
Student:
ID or Alpha Code:
Grade:
Academic Evaluations
Attendance Concerns/Letters
Behavior Documents
    Positive Behavior Improvement Pan
    Functional Behavior Assessment
    Developmental History
    Multi-Tier System of Supports/Problem Solving Team Plan

Conference notes from meeting within the last 2 years
    Fidelity Logs for interventions
    Last year _____ Current year_____
    Graphed data (from last meeting)
Psychological testing (past 2 years)
    Section 504 Plan
    Current Plan
    Eligibility/Ineligibility documentation
    Dismissal documentation
Other:
It is our hope that the requested documents be made available for pick-up with 72 hours. If this is not reasonable, please contact me via phone _____.
Sincerely,

References

Henderson, A., & Mapp, K. (2002). *A new wave of evidence: The impact of school, family, and community connections on student achievement.* Austin, TX: Southwest Educational Development Laboratory.

Ho Sui-Chu, E., & Willms, J. D. (1996). Effects of parental involvement on eighth-grade achievement. Sociology of Education, 69(2), 126–141.

Lopez, M. Elena, & Caspe, Margaret. (2014). Family engagement in anywhere, anytime learning. Family Involvement Network of Educators (FINE) Newsletter, 6(3). Retrieved from http://www.hfrp.org/publications-resources/browse-our-publications/family-engagement-in-anywhere-anytime-learning

Mapp, K. (2004). Family engagement. In F. P. Schargel & J. Smink (Eds), *Helping students graduate: A strategic approach to dropout prevention (pp. 99-113). Larchmont, NY: Eye on Education.*

National Parent Teacher Organization. (2002). PTA National Standards for Family-School Partnerships: An Implementation Guide.

www.pta.org/files/National_Standards_Implementation_Guide_2009.pdf

Wilson, B., & Corbett, D. H. (2000). "I didn't know I could do that": Parents learning to be leaders through the Commonwealth Institute for Parent Leadership. Lexington, KY: Commonwealth Institute for Parent Leadership. http://www.cipl.org/pubs.html

Meet the Author

Timothy King is the founder of Crowning Moments, a consulting company with concentrations in Education, Ministry, and Leadership. He is the District Discipline and Behavior Coordinator for Flagler County Schools, located in Palm Coast, FL. He has 18 years of educational experience ranging from paraprofessional to district level administration, where he is currently responsible for the development of the Student Code of Conduct, writing discipline policy and protocol, implementing new policy and training, and monitoring of discipline data. He holds certifications in Elementary Education, Special Education (K-12), and Principal/School leader (K-12).

Crowning Moments
PO Box 352504
Palm Coast, FL 32135
(386) 227-7628
www.crowningmomentsconsultants.com

www.ingramcontent.com/pod-product-compliance
Lightning Source LLC
Chambersburg PA
CBHW070041070426
42449CB00012BA/3131